Presented to

_____

On the occasion of

_____

From

_____

Date

_____

Friends

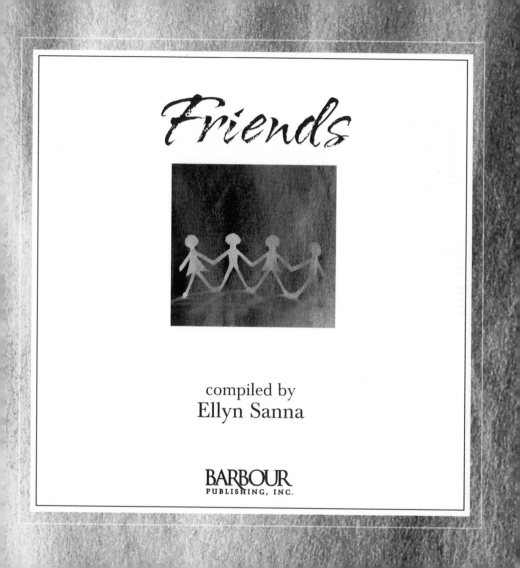

compiled by
Ellyn Sanna

BARBOUR
PUBLISHING, INC.

Published by Barbour Publishing, Inc., P.O. Box 719, Uhrichsville, Ohio 44683
http://www.barbourbooks.com

Member of the
Evangelical Christian
Publishers Association

Printed in China.

Friends

Life's Best Treasure

Ointment and perfume rejoice the heart:
so doth the sweetness of a man's friend by hearty counsel.
Iron sharpeneth iron;
so a man sharpeneth the countenance of his friend.
PROVERBS 27:9, 17 (KJV)

*People who have
warm friends
are healthier and
happier than those
who have none.
A single real friend
is a treasure worth
more than gold or
precious stones.
Money can buy
many things, good
and evil. All the
wealth of the world
could not buy you a
friend or pay you
for the loss of one.*
G. D. PRENTICE

*Our treasured friendships shape who
we become in life. . .*

I was an oddball child. We lived in
the country, so I never had neighbors
with whom I played, and even at school I
never quite fit in. I spent my days in the
companionship of imaginary
friends: an imaginary stable of horses,
imaginary husbands (two of them!), and
an imaginary grandmother. But even my
imaginary friends weren't my own age,
and when I was nine I began to long for a
friend my own age, someone like me. I
stopped wishing on stars for a baby
brother, and began to wish for a friend.

That same year my friend Joyce
moved to our school, and the year after
my friend Patty came. At last, I had
friends, and life was no longer quite so
lonely. But by junior high, both Patty and

Joyce had steady boyfriends, and I was alone again. This time I didn't wish on stars; instead, I began to pray that God would send me someone I could talk to.

I was tired of being different from everyone else. While all the other girls my age were going steady or dreaming over Sean Cassidy, I was daydreaming about Heathcliff; while they listened to Rod Stewart and Jethro Tull, I was listening to Tchaikovsky. While they went to dances and giggled over boys, I was reading Tolkien and writing my own fantasy. I tried to pretend I was like all the others; I even made up a boyfriend to talk about. But I had an uneasy feeling in my middle whenever I talked about him. I wished I could just be myself.

And then at a pajama party one weekend, I met a tiny girl named Pam. She had wispy brown hair, small oval glasses, and her face was so small, I didn't think she could be my own age. She was, though, but she was different from the other thirteen-year-olds I knew. While the others stayed up talking about boys and scary baby-sitter stories, Pam and I made up our own stories about talking animals; we pretended and talked all night long. At last, I thought blissfully as I finally fell asleep the next morning, someone who can still play.

After that, life was different. Now I had someone who read the same books I did, someone who thought about the same things. We would lie on our backs looking up at the stars, talking about God and space and time travel. We wrote letters to each other with quill pens, pretending to be Jessica and Arabel, two girls who had lived in the nineteen hundreds. We went to the library together every day after school, and on the weekends we went for long walks in the woods, telling each other stories about magical lands.

I'm sure one way or another I would have survived my adolescence even without Pam. But her friendship allowed me to stay a little longer in childhood's world of wonder and magic. . .and her encouragement gave me the strength to take that wonder with me as I crossed the line into adulthood.

The day I met Pam, God gave me one of my life's greatest treasures.

If you want an accounting of your worth, count your friends.
MERRY BROWNE

There is no folly equal to that of throwing away friendship,
in a world where friendship is so rare.

BULWER-LYTTON

A good friend is better than. . .
- any promotion or raise.
- inheriting a million dollars.
- a diamond ring.
- a new car.
- being the president of anything.

The comfort of having a friend may be taken away,
but not that of having had one.

SENECA

*The best that
we find
in our travels
is an
honest friend.
He is a
fortunate
voyager
who
finds many.*

ROBERT
LOUIS STEVENSON

Imagine what life would be like without your friends. No one to call when you have a fight with your husband. No one with whom to share coffee and laughter. No one to cry with you when everything is going wrong, no one to be glad for you when everything is going right. No one with whom to share your thoughts, no one to pray for you.

Thank God for your friends. We can get by without money and prestige and new possessions—but the thought of getting by without our friends is too painful to imagine. They are truly one of life's greatest treasures.

*Of our mixed life two quests are
given control; Food for the body,
friendship for the soul.*

ARTHUR UPSON

We are the weakest of spendthrifts if we let one friend drop off through inattention, or let one push away another, or if we hold aloof from one for petty jealousy or heedless roughness. Would you throw away a diamond because it pricked you? One good friend is not to be weighed against all the jewels of the earth.

WILL CARLETON

True happiness
Consists not in the multitude of friends,
But in their worth and choice.
BEN JONSON

If instead of a gem, or even a flower,
we should cast the gift of rich thought into the heart of a friend,
that would be giving as the angels give.
GEORGE MACDONALD

Friendship, like leisure, is often sacrificed on the altar of pragmatic concerns. Because keeping in touch with cherished friends is not as pressing as getting the shopping or the office report done, it is usually put off to another time. Unfortunately, convenient times for fostering friendships become less and less as the pace of our life quickens. Friendship for Christians cannot be viewed as a frill that gets eliminated when time and resources shrink. The spiritual journey requires close friends. . . . Jesus sent the disciples out on their missionary journey in pairs so that their companionship would be a support, especially in those inhospitable towns from which they were advised to leave after shaking the dust from their sandals.

WILKIE AU,
BY WAY OF THE HEART

Rings and jewels are not gifts, but apologies for gifts.
The only gift is a portion of thyself.
RALPH WALDO EMERSON

Dear God, thank You for my friends.
Help me not to take them for granted.
Sometimes my priorities get twisted up
so easily; I start thinking that money
and possessions are more important
than people. Your Son's life shows me
that You treasure individuals far more than
You care about earthly prestige or power or
wealth. Remind me often how poor my life would be without the
friends You've given me. Help me to enrich their lives as they
have mine. Amen.

The Gift
of a Friend's Love

This is my command: Love each other.
JOHN 15:17 (NIV)

*The greatest
happiness of life
is the conviction
that we are loved,
loved for ourselves,
or rather loved
in spite of ourselves.*
VICTOR HUGO

Love is a virtue because it demonstrates patience rather than petulance, responds with kindness when confronted by the failures of others, and goes out of its way to contribute to the needs of others, even at its own expense. As the apostle Paul said in concluding his hymn in praise of love, "It bears all things, believes all things, hopes all things, endures all things. Love never ends" (1 Cor. 13:7–8 RSV).

. . .Love is the jewel in the crown of virtues that belongs to those who seek and find the joys of balanced spirituality. "Pursue love and strive for the spiritual gifts," urges Paul (1 Cor. 14:1).

Love never ends, it is never finished, it never speaks the last word, it never reaches a conclusion that is not also a beginning.

RAY S. ANDERSON,
LIVING THE SPIRITUALLY BALANCED LIFE

Friendship is an education. It draws the friend out of himself and all that is selfish and ignoble in him and leads him to life's higher levels of altruism and sacrifice. Many a man has been saved from a life of frivolity and emptiness to a career of noble service by finding at a critical hour the right kind of friend.

G. D. PRENTICE

I know my friends love me because. . .
- they listen to me complain about my life.
- they're proud of me when I do a good job.
- they put up with all my bad habits.
- they laugh at my jokes.
- they believe in me even when no one else does.

If a friend is in trouble, don't annoy him by asking if there is anything you can do. Think up something appropriate and do it.
EDGAR WATSON HOWE

Among those whom I like, I can find no common denominator,
but among those whom I love, I can:
all of them make me laugh.
W. H. AUDEN

Love is a choice—not simply,
or necessarily a rational choice,
but rather a willingness
to be present to others
without pretense or guile.
CARTER HEYWARD

The most human thing we have to do in life is to learn to
speak our honest convictions and feelings and live with the
consequences. This is the first requirement of love.
WILLIAM DU BAY

Sometimes, the best way for a friend to give her love is silently, without any words at all...

A few years ago I had to have a surgery that would mean I would never again be able to have children. I tried to be brave and rational and practical; after all, I had three wonderful children, so how could I complain? But inside my heart I was full of darkness; no matter how much I smiled on the outside, anger and sorrow tumbled around inside me like a load of heavy rocks.

My friends with children all told me how much better I'd feel once I had my surgery; I smiled and agreed. They told me that three children were all anyone could want; again, I smiled and nodded. They told me how lucky I was to have had my children after years of miscarriages; many women, they reminded me,

The most I can do for my friend is simply to be his friend. I have no wealth to bestow upon him. If he knows that I am happy in loving him he will want no other reward. Is not friendship divine in this?

LAVATIN

had not been blessed as I had been. I agreed with everything they said, of course I did. So I had no choice but to hide my tears.

Only Lois, my friend who has no children, touched my hand and said nothing. On the day of the surgery, she was there at the hospital with my husband, a strong loving presence for us both. Afterward, in a haze of anesthesia and pain, I found she had left me a present: a small gift bag, two angels printed on its bright sides, waited for me on the hospital table. I was too weak to reach for it, too sick to really understand even that it was a gift for me, but I did know that Lois had left it there. All night the angels' rose and gold faces seemed to look at me lovingly through the darkness.

In the morning, I was enough myself again that I reached for the gift bag. For a moment I simply held it in my lap, thinking that there was no gift I wanted, no present that could possibly make up for the emptiness I felt. I sighed and tipped the bag over.

Three green wooden hearts tumbled out onto the bed, a big one, a medium one, a small one. Tole painting edged their curves, and their simple beauty pleased me. I turned them over then and realized they each bore the name of one of my children.

Something inside me broke open. I was not empty after all, I realized, and no matter what life brought me, I knew I never would be. How could I be, when my lap was full of little hearts?

$Love$ is extravagant in the price it is willing to pay, the time it is willing to give, the hardships it is willing to endure, and the strength it is willing to spend.

Love never thinks in terms of "how little," but always in terms of "how much."

JONI EARECKSON TADA,
SECRET STRENGTH

There are no rules for friendship.
It must be left to itself.
We cannot force it any more than love.
WILLIAM HAZLITT

However rare true love is, true friendship is rarer.
LA ROCHEFOUCAULD

Friendship cheers like a sunbeam; charms like a good story; inspires like a brave leader; binds like a golden chain; guides like a heavenly vision.

Happy is the house that shelters a friend! . . . I awoke this morning with devout thanksgiving for my friends, the old and the new. . . . High thanks I owe you, excellent lovers, who carry out the world for me to new and noble depths, and enlarge the meaning of all my thoughts. . . .

There are two elements that go to the composition of friendship, each so sovereign that I can detect no superiority in either, no reason why either should be first named. One is truth. A friend is a person with whom I can be sincere. Before him I may think aloud. I. . .may deal with him with the simplicity and wholeness with which one atom meets another. . . .

The other element of friendship is tenderness. . . . The only way to have a friend is to be one. . . .

RALPH WALDO EMERSON

A brother may not be a friend,
but a friend will always be a brother.
BENJAMIN FRANKLIN

*I don't meddle
with what my friends believe or reject,
any more than I ask whether
they are rich or poor; I love them.*
JAMES RUSSELL LOWELL

I never considered a difference of opinion in politics,
in religion, in philosophy, as cause
for withdrawing from a friend.
THOMAS JEFFERSON

> *The true friend seeks to give, not to take; to help, not to be helped; to minister, not to be ministered unto.*
>
> WILLIAM RADER

He who would grow into larger and richer friendships must recognize first of all that, if his friend is in truth worthy of such a friendship as he seeks, the great way is by personal association. One cannot grab up and hurry off with the fine fruits of friendship. No friendship that counts for much with either men or God can become one's own without the giving of time, of thought, of attention, of honest response. . . . No friendship is so high, so fine, or so assured that it does not need that the friends should take time to be together, that they should be willing to think enough to enter with some appreciation into the thought and experience of each other, and that they should make honest response to the best in each other's character and in each other's vision.

HENRY C. KING

It is chance that makes brothers, but hearts that make friends.

E. VON GEIBEL

God has given us two hands—one to receive
with and the other to give with.
We are not cisterns made for hoarding;
we are channels made for giving.

BILLY GRAHAM

Dear God, thank You for all the love You give me
through my friends. So many times I have felt You touch me
through their loving hands. Help me to return their love—not just
inside my heart, but in practical ways they can touch and see.
Make my life a gift of love. Amen.

We must strengthen, defend, preserve and comfort each other.
We must love one another.

JOHN WINTHROP

Hearts that Understand

Out of the abundance of the heart the mouth speaketh.
MATTHEW 12:34 (KJV)

A friend is a person
with whom you dare to be yourself.
FRANK CRANE

*The language of friendship is not words,
but meanings.
It is an intelligence above language.*
HENRY DAVID THOREAU

A true test of friendship–
to sit or walk with a friend
for an hour in perfect silence
without wearying of one another's company.
DINAH MULOCK CRAIK

Friendship arises out of mere Companionship when two or more of the companions discover that they have in common some insight or interest or even taste which the others do not share and which, till that moment, each believed to be his own unique treasure (or burden). The typical expression of opening Friendship would be something like, "What? You too? I thought I was the only one."

. . .That is why those pathetic people who simply "want friends" can never make any. The very condition of having Friends is that we should want something else besides Friends. Where the truthful answer to the question "Do you see the same truth?" would be "I see nothing and I don't care about the truth; I only want a Friend," no Friendship can arise—though Affection of course may. There would be nothing for the Friendship to be about; and Friendship must be about something, even if it were only an enthusiasm for dominoes or white mice. Those who have nothing can share nothing; those who are going nowhere can have no fellow-travelers.

C.S. LEWIS, , *THE FOUR LOVES*

One of the most beautiful qualities
of true friendship is to understand and to be understood.
SENECA

*B*ut, after all, the very best thing in good talk, and the thing that helps most, is friendship. How it dissolves the barriers that divide us, and loosens all constraint, and diffuses itself like some fine old cordial through all the veins of life—this feeling that we understand and trust each other, and wish each other heartily well! Everything into which it really comes is good.

HENRY VAN DYKE

We want but two or three friends, but these we cannot do without, and they serve us in every thought we think.

RALPH WALDO EMERSON

When Zeno was asked what a friend was,
he replied, "Another I."
DIOGENES

You know you're really friends when. . .
- you can talk to each other every day
  and never run out of things to say.
- you don't have to clean the house for each other.
- you know each other's secrets.
- the same things make you laugh.
- you can count on each other to always tell the truth.

Friendship is like two clocks keeping time.
UNKNOWN

*Almost
any friend
will sympathize
with you
over the
really big
things in life—
but the friend
who really
understands
is the one
who gives you
sympathy
for even the
most trivial
sorrows.*

As a stay-at-home mom who also works full time, sometimes I get a little desperate. Back when I had kids at home all day, my friend Tammy listened daily to my frustrations. "Get a baby-sitter," she advised. "You'll enjoy your children more if you have just two or three afternoons a week when you can work uninterrupted."

At last, I decided to take her advice. But finding a baby-sitter was no easy task. One young woman said she could do it. . .as long as her boyfriend could come with her. Another wanted to give it a try. . .except she could only come once a week. Still another thought it might be a fun job. . .if I would pay her double what she could make at McDonalds. "When we were teenagers, weren't we desperate for a job?" I complained to Tammy.

She encouraged me not to give up. . .and at last, after weeks had gone by, I found a teenage girl who would work the hours I needed her at the pay I could give her. The first two days she came, I sailed out to the library, my briefcase under my arm, with a sense of freedom. I found that three hours of work surrounded by peace and quiet were nearly as good as a full day's work surrounded by preschoolers.

"Thank you," I told Tammy. "Thank you for not letting me give up. It was worth all the trouble it took to find a baby-sitter."

On the third day, however, the baby-sitter stopped me as I was going out the door. "This is the last day I can come, Mrs. Sanna," she said sweetly. "I'm going to be starting dance rehearsals next week and I also have another baby-sitting job."

Friendship maketh daylight in the understanding, out of darkness and confusion of thoughts.
FRANCIS BACON

I stood very still, my hand on the door-knob. I sucked in a deep breath. "All right," I choked and went out the door.

Driving down the street away from my house, I was overwhelmed with discouragement. I knew I couldn't concentrate on my work. Not until I told Tammy. . . As I passed a pay phone, I pulled over. Quickly, I dialed the number I knew so well. As soon as I heard her voice I started to cry.

"What is it?" she asked, frightened by my sobs.

I poured out my pathetic story, unable to hold back the tears. And Tammy didn't tell me to get a grip or remind me that I'd lost my sense of perspective or imply that maybe I needed to grow up. I did need to get a grip, and I had lost my sense of perspective, and I probably did need to grow up—but she just listened and let me know she understood.

I never did find another baby-sitter. But every day until my kids were finally all in school Tammy listened to my frustrations. No disappointment was ever too small for me to tell her, no accomplishment too trivial to share with her. When we lost our tempers with our children, we sympathized with each other. . . and when we finally cleaned our basements, we were proud of each other. I knew that whatever was going on in my life, Tammy would understand—and because she did, I could always get a grip again on the pieces of my life. Talking with her, I'd regain my sense of perspective and start to laugh at myself. Maybe I even grew up a little.

Being with people you like and respect is so meaningful. Perhaps you have known some of them most of your life. Having friends around for a pleasant evening is one of life's most cherished joys as far as I am concerned. But when those with me are fellow believers how much greater that joy is, for we know that it will be rekindled, one day, in eternity.

JAMES STEWART

Dear God, thank You for understanding friends. Thank You that so often we're on the same wavelength, laughing together, crying together, encouraging each other with our understanding. I'm grateful that I'm not alone, that I can share my life with my friends. And when I listen to them, give me a heart that understands. Amen.

Knowing is the most profound kind of love, giving someone the gift of knowledge about yourself.
MARSHA NORMAN

Therefore if there is any encouragement in Christ, if there is any consolation of love, if there is any fellowship of the Spirit, if any affection and compassion, make my joy complete by being of the same mind, maintaining the same love, united in spirit, intent on one purpose.

PHILIPPIANS 2:1–2 (NASB)

Love is patient, love is kind. It does not envy, it does not boast, it is not proud. It is not rude, it is not self-seeking, it is not easily angered, it keeps no record of wrongs.

1 CORINTHIANS 13:4–5 (NIV)

True friends don't spend time gazing into each other's eyes.
They show great tenderness toward each other,
but they face in the same direction—
toward common projects, interests, goals—
above all,
toward a common Lord.
C. S. LEWIS

Friendship. . .is an Union of Spirits,
a Marriage of Hearts.
WILLIAM PENN

Sharing Joy, Sharing Sorrow

So encourage each other to build each other up,
just as you are already doing.
1 Thessalonians 5:11 (TLB)

Friendship renders prosperity more brilliant,
while it lightens adversity by sharing it
and making its burden common.

CICERO

A good friend. . .
- makes a hot fudge sundae taste even better.
- calms us down when we're angry.
- shares our tears.
- laughs at the same things we do.
- prays for us when we're too weak to pray for ourselves.

"Unbosom yourself," said Wimsey.
"Trouble shared is trouble halved."

DOROTHY SAYERS

A Soul Friend

I met Carolyn years ago at my first job. She was sixteen years older than I—not quite old enough to be a mother figure, but almost. As we shared our faith and got to know each other, she quickly became my mentor. . .and as the years went by, I came to think of her as my "soul friend."

Late at night, we would sit together in her quiet living room and talk about our lives. She was the one who advised me on matters of the heart as I fumbled through my first serious relationship with a man. And she was the one who cried with me when that relationship ended in heartbreak. She encouraged me when I went to a new job and listened to my fears and failures as I struggled with its challenges. She rejoiced with me when I fell in love again, and she sat up with me on the night before my

Two are better than one. . . . If one falls down, his friend can help him up. But pity the man who falls and has no one to help him up!
ECCLESIASTES 4:9–10 (NIV)

wedding. We talked and laughed as I put the finishing touches on the veil I had made myself—and when I stuck my feet to the floor with Crazy Glue, she rescued me. When I was with her, I always seemed to soak up serenity, as though the Holy Spirit flowed quietly between us.

But as I began my married life, she and her family moved across the country. Once or twice a month we would talk on the phone, but those long distance calls just weren't the same as when we daily shared our joys and sorrows.

> *We have been friends together in sunshine and shade.*
> CAROLINE NORTON

Then came the dark time in my life when I lost three babies in a row. Carolyn sent me flowers and cards; I knew that even on the other side of the continent she loved and cared for me. But something inside me was frozen solid. I walked around, I went to work, I talked and laughed. . .but I could not pray. The months went by, and everyone expected me to be "all better." No one wanted to hear about the miscarriages that still absorbed so much of my thoughts.

Then an opportunity came for me to visit Carolyn, and all alone I flew across the country. I hadn't seen in her in so long that

I felt a little shy, but as she showed me around her new house, I touched the familiar things that made me feel at home. After her family was all in bed, we sat down and began to talk.

"Tell me about the miscarriages," she said.

For the first time, I shared everything that had happened: the physical pain and fear and blood, the sorrow and emptiness and anger. There in her quiet living room, we cried together. . .and as she took my sorrow and made it her own, I found it was no longer so dark and overwhelming. She helped me see the joy hidden in the shadows. Softly, she began to pray out loud for me. . . and I felt my heart melt, soaking up the Spirit's peace as He moved between us.

To have joy one must share it—
Happiness was born a twin.
LORD BYRON

*Good friends help us find
the adventure in life. . .*

College was one of the best times of my life. The friends I had there were the closest I've ever had, before or since. Probably part of the reason for that was that we took the place of family for each other. We were family. Oh, we had our petty squabbles and our actual fights, but just like in a family, things generally seemed to work out. We could be real with each other, show our true selves. Being together made everything seem better, brighter, more exciting.

Just before final exams one year, six of us drove up to Toronto on a whim. By the time we made the three-hour trip, it was dark, and we had no idea what to do there. We especially didn't know what we could do without much money; we were poor college students after all. We left the car in a parking garage near the downtown area, deciding we might as well walk around and see what there was to see.

We looked around the base of the CN Tower, but it was much too expensive for us to even think of riding the elevator to the top. The SkyDome looked interesting, but there was no game on that night, not to mention that money would have been a problem again. Then we found a mall, but it was late; all the stores were closed.

So we spent hours walking up and down one of the main streets of Toronto, not doing anything but walking and being together. That didn't really bother us, though; we had fun anyway. I think we could have had fun anywhere, but a new and different location was something memorable. We were amazed by how many other people were walking around downtown at midnight, all of them talking and laughing just like we were.

"Remember when we went to Toronto?" we'd ask each other later.

"What did you do?" people would ask us. "Did you go shopping? Go to a baseball game? See a musical?"

We would look at each other and shrug. "We just walked around really. But we had a lot of fun."

"You didn't do anything at all?"

"Well, we talked and looked at things." We couldn't really explain why we had so much fun; that was just the way things seemed to be when we were together.

Being together made everything seem like an adventure. It could be going to Toronto. . .but watching a movie together could be almost as much fun. . .or going to the grocery store. . .or even the hardware store. It was even an adventure when I broke my thumb skiing and my friends had to take me to the emergency room. Wherever we were, we talked and laughed and were fascinated by everything we saw. We talked about anything and everything, serious or ridiculous, intellectual or completely frivolous. We were a family.

Since graduation, we've pretty much scattered across the country and around the world. But when we get together, it's almost as though nothing has changed. As I share the events of my life, I find the excitement I sometimes overlook now. Disappointments don't seem so important, and the joys seem even greater. Everything seems like an adventure.

SHEILA STEWART
(USED WITH THE AUTHOR'S PERMISSION)

Friendships multiply joys, and divide griefs.
H. G. BOHN

Dear God, I am grateful for the friends who participate in both my joys and sorrows. My discouragement is never so overwhelming when my friends help me carry it, and I find meaning even in my life's greatest sorrows. Laughter shared is twice as hilarious, and I take the deepest satisfaction in my life's blessing when I share them with my friends. Thank You for giving us the ability to communicate our feelings to each other; thank You for sending Your Spirit to us through our friends.

*Carry
each other's
burdens,
and in this way
you will
fulfill the law
of Christ.*
GALATIANS 6:2 (NIV)

A Friend's Forgiveness

Be kind and compassionate to one another,
forgiving each other, just as in Christ God forgave you.
EPHESIANS 4:32 (NIV)

When two friends part they should lock up each other's secrets
and exchange keys. The truly noble mind has no resentments.

DIOGENES

*He who throws away a friend
is as bad as he who throws away his life.*

SOPHOCLES

A true friend forgives you even when. . .
- you forget her birthday.
- you act like a brat when she forgets your birthday.
- you stand her up for a lunch date two times in a row.
- you borrow her favorite jacket and spill tomato sauce on it.
- you can't stop talking about the fight you had with your mother,
  even though you know she wants to talk about her new job.

Forgiveness is a choice you make. . . . If you don't forgive, it brings death into your life in one form or another. The best way to become forgiving is to pray for the person you need to forgive.

STORMIE OMARTIAN

Maybe we remember the few occasions in our life in which we were able to show someone we love our real self: not only our great successes but also our weaknesses and pains, not only our good intentions but also our bitter motives, not only our radiant face but also our dark shadow. . . .

Loving is not based on the willingness to listen, to understand problems of others, or to tolerate their otherness. Love is based on the mutuality of the confession of our total self to each other. This makes us free to declare not only: "My strength is your strength" but also: "Your pain is my pain, your weakness is my weakness. . . ." It is in this intimate exposure of one's deepest dependency that love is born.

HENRI J. M. NOUWEN,
INTIMACY

*Our commitment to forgive each other
no matter what makes friendships
last forever. . .*

I'm not very good at writing letters. I mean to write them; as I'm driving or when I'm lying in bed at night, I always compose them in my mind. But somehow, for all that I make my living writing words, I seldom seem to take the time for my correspondence. Between my children and my career, there never seems to be enough little spaces left for writing letters.

Year after year, though, my friend Joyce forgives me. I've been friends with her since we were kids, and her commitment to our friendship is one of the solid rocks in my life. She lives across the country now, and if we're lucky we see each other once a year—but Joyce keeps us close all year long with her letters.

Her letters are always long and full of

everything that's been happening in her heart. For every three or four she writes, one of mine finds its way back to her, but her stream of correspondence never falters. Her forgiveness for my silence never seems to falter either. With her letters she lets me know that no matter how old we get or where we go in life, we will always be friends. She sent me a book once about the correspondence between two friends, a book called *Touchstones,* and since then I often think of her friendship as a touchstone in my life.

A touchstone was once used as a test for gold; when it was scratched, it revealed a metal's worth. My busyness, my life's over-commitment, my lack of discipline sometimes scrape against my friendship with Joyce—but they reveal the solid gold that remains at our friendship's heart. This is a true friendship, a friendship to treasure for a lifetime. . .and her forgiveness heals the scrapes and scratches, and keeps our friendship growing.

Two persons cannot long be friends
if they cannot forgive each other's little failings.
JEAN DE LA BRUYÈRE

$\mathcal{D}o$ not be sensitive. Perhaps you are by nature, but you can get over it with the exercise of common sense and the help of God. Let things hurt until the tender spot gets callous. . . . Sensitiveness is only another kind of self-consciousness, and as such we should seek deliverance from its irritating power.

ISABELLA THOBURN

Every man **should** have a
fair-sized **cemetery**
in which to **bury the** faults
of his **friends.**
HENRY WARD BEECHER

My friend is not perfect—nor am I—
and so we suit each other admirably.
ALEXANDER POPE

Dear God, help me to forgive my friends when they seem to let me down. Remind me that only You are perfect; only You can always be there and always understand me. Thank You for all the times my friends forgive me. I never seem to use up their forgiveness; thank You for showing Your own nature through them. Amen.

I like a friend the better
for having faults that one can talk about.
WILLIAM HAZLITT

Then came Peter to him, and said, Lord,
how oft shall my brother sin against me, and I forgive him?
till seven times? Jesus saith unto him, I say not unto thee,
Until seven times: but, Until seventy times seven.
MATTHEW 18:21–22 (KJV)

Old Friends

I thank my God every time I remember you.
PHILIPPIANS 1:3 (NIV)

Time draweth wrinkles in a fair face, but addeth fresh colors
to a fast friend, which neither heat, nor cold, nor misery,
nor place, nor destiny, can alter or diminish.

JOHN LYLY

As gold more splendid from the fire appears,
Thus friendship brightens by the length of years.

THOMAS CARLYLE

An old friend is someone who. . .
• remembers what you looked like in seventh grade.
• knows the name of the first boy you loved.
• doesn't tell your children all the rules you broke
    when you were a teenager.
• knows a few things about you that even
    your husband doesn't know.
• has known you through all the changes in your life—
    and still loves you.

Nothing is as comfortable as an old friend. . .

The first time I met Patty was in fifth grade; she had straight blonde hair that stuck out around her face and her glasses were blue and pointed. She was nervous and edgy and kind to everyone; I thought she was wonderful.

Thirty years later I still think she's wonderful. Over the years, we've talked about most everything, from God to sex and back again; we've shared our crazy fears and laughed at ourselves; we've cried with each other and prayed for each other and complimented each other's new hairstyles. We know each other's wounds and weaknesses. We understand each other, because we were there when we were each being shaped; we remember our childhood sorrows and teenage agonies.

We can talk once a week on the phone, or once a month, or once every three months, and it never seems to matter: Things are always the same between us. No one has ever made me laugh more.

The wonderful thing about an old friend like Patty is you never have to explain where you're coming from. She already knows.

For believe me, in this world,
which is ever slipping
from under our feet,
it is the prerogative of friendship
to grow old with one's friends.

ARTHUR S. HARDY

There is no friend like the old friend
   who has shared our morning days,
No greeting like his welcome,
   no homage like his praise;
Fame is the scentless sunflower,
   with a gaudy crown of gold;
But friendship is the breathing rose,
   with sweets in every fold.

OLIVER WENDELL HOLMES

Dear God, thank You for my old friends. I'm grateful for their faithful friendship. Thank You for the comfort they give me when the world seems overwhelming. Thank You for the laughter they've brought into my life over the years. I'm glad our friendship will last into eternity. Amen.

There is no better looking-glass than an old friend.
THOMAS FULLER

There are evergreen men and women in the world, praise be to God!—not many of them, but a few. The sun of our prosperity makes the green of their friendship no brighter, the frost of our adversity kills not the leaves of their affection.
JEROME K. JEROME

New Friends

I was a stranger, and ye took me in.

MATTHEW 25:35 (KJV)

We do not make friends as we make houses,
but discover them as we do the arbutus,
under the leaves of our lives, concealed in our experience.

WILLIAM RADER

You know you've made a new friend when. . .
- you find yourselves laughing at the same jokes.
- you discover you like the same books and movies.
- you find yourselves talking faster and faster,
    trying to find out everything about each other.
- you realize you share the same faith in God.
- the differences you find only make
    the other person seem more interesting.

When one helps another, both are strong.

GERMAN PROVERB

I spent a Saturday last year in a
strange city, running a book stand at a
Christian conference. A friend of a friend,
a woman named Gerry who lived nearby,
would be there to help me, but I had
never met her before, and I was dreading
a long day alone away from my family. I
was tired, spiritually dry, overwhelmed by
all the responsibilities that were piling up
around me; the last thing I wanted to do
was spend a day with a stranger.

As I waited for Gerry to arrive, I had a
clear mental picture of what she would
look like—older than I, a little dowdy, stout,
wearing a shapeless print dress and sensi-
ble shoes. I watched for her anxiously,
eager to go get a cup of coffee once she
was there to watch the book stand. I barely
noticed the woman who stalked by me

> *Blessed are they
> who have the gift
> of making friends,
> for it is one
> of God's best gifts.
> It involves
> many things,
> but above all
> the power of going
> out of one's self,
> and appreciating
> what is noble and
> loving in another.*
> THOMAS HUGHES

twice, dressed in blue jeans and boots and a leather jacket. She finally shook back her mane of thick dark curls and asked, "Are you Ellyn?"

Well, she was older than me. I could only hope I would look as good when I was her age. I eyed her sideways as we sold books together, wondering about her. We smiled at each other and made polite conversation.

And then at some point in that long day we started talking. First, we talked about the books we were selling. And then we talked about other books we had read, and we found we'd been reading the same things. We started to talk about God and discovered that spiritually we were on the same page. We talked about our sisters and our nieces; we talked about our old boyfriends and our mothers and growing up. We realized that we had somehow reached very similar places in our lives, even though we had taken different routes to get there. The day flew by. We couldn't talk fast enough, couldn't

> *How can we tell what coming people are aboard the ships that may be sailing to us now from the unknown seas?*
> CHARLES DICKENS

hide our delight at finding someone who understood exactly what we meant.

At the end of the day, she helped me load the books back in their boxes. We hugged and said good-bye—and I knew even if I never saw her again, I had made a friend. Her friendship encouraged me, made my responsibilities seem less overwhelming; I found I remembered the things in my life that excited me. I felt challenged to go further on my journey with God.

I didn't sell many books that day—but I went home a little richer.

Dear God, thank You for the new friends
You send into my life. Help me never to think I have all the
friends I need. Remind me that You have new ways to touch me
through each person that I meet. Amen.

*Even Across
the Miles*

*May the Lord keep watch between you
and me when we are away from each other.*
GENESIS 31:49 (NIV)

Nothing makes the earth seem so spacious as to have friends at a distance: they make the latitudes and longitudes.

HENRY DAVID THOREAU

*Even across the miles,
true friends stay in touch with each other by. . .*

talking on the phone.

writing letters.

sending e-mail.

remembering.

praying.

What joy is better than the news of friends?

ROBERT BROWNING

Dear Father,

Today Darla told me she's moving. It seems like yesterday she caught my bridal bouquet. I still smile when I think that it wasn't even a year later I was in her wedding. That was a special time for me. I was a treasured friend standing at the altar with her sisters.

Her new home is a forty-hour drive away. That's definitely too far for a tea party. It's too far for meeting at the playground. Who will share goals and dreams with me while we watch our children swing? We won't be scheduling racquetball games or tee times for our husbands. I'll have to find someone else for hand-me-down clothes. Maybe I'll visit the new quilt store alone.

I'll give you the desires of your heart.

But this is as painful as when LouAnne, my other kindred friend, moved. It's been five long years, and I still miss her. I remember

Even miles can't separate kindred friends.

when she became pregnant, how excited we were at the miracle You had wrought. But LouAnne moved before her baby was born, and I never even held him. He'll be starting school this fall.

I finally had the courage to walk past her house. I even met the family living there. But we're not kindred friends.

My ways are greater than your ways.

You've given me two kindred friends. Our relationships are deeper than common interests and experiences; they're more than coffee breaks, PTA meetings, or even Bible studies. We share our dreams and disappointments. It takes more than time to develop that kind of friendship. How will I ever find another kindred friend?

Begin with Me.

A kindred friend is someone I'm so comfortable with, we're like a pair of worn slippers. She's a friend I call on when my husband travels and I'm afraid.

Call on Me.

She's a friend I can depend on whenever I'm down in the dumps.

Trust Me.

Father, it seems that all my kindred friends relocate to the other side of the country. Is it because You're a jealous God who wants us to depend only on You? Was I starting to depend too much on my friends instead of You?

Depend on Me.

I trust You. But I'll still miss my friend.

You will remain forever friends across the miles. But there's a woman across the country who also needs a kindred spirit. Can you accept that another needs your friend's

She accepts me as I am. It doesn't matter how I look or if my home is messy. She isn't upset if I'm a few minutes late or early. We encourage each other, motivate each other. We're one another's confidants. I trust her with my fears. I know she won't reject me even if I disappoint her.

companionship now?

    This isn't easy, Father. But yes. Yes, I can. Thank You for letting me share my kindred friend across the miles.

DONNA LANGE

(USED WITH THE AUTHOR'S PERMISSION)

Thou goest thy way and I go mine;
Apart, yet not afar;
Only a thin veil hangs between
The pathways where we are;
And "God keep watch 'tween thee and me,"
This is my prayer;
He looks thy way. He looketh mine.
And keeps us near.

JULIA A. BAKER

Dear God, be with my friends even
when we can't be together. Thank You
that miles have no meaning in eternity. Amen.

*As cold waters
to a thirsty soul,
so is good news
from a far country.*
PROVERBS 25:25 (KJV)

A Glimpse of God

No one has ever seen God; but if we love one other,
God lives in us and his love is made complete in us.
<small>1 JOHN 4:12 (NIV)</small>

Every true friend is a glimpse of God.

LUCY LARCOM

Our friends are like God when they. . .
- stick by us through all the changes in our lives.
- forgive us over and over.
- never stop listening and caring and understanding.
- give themselves to us.
- love us no matter what.

The more we love, the better we are;
and the greater our friendships are, the dearer we are to God.

JEREMY TAYLOR

A secret Master of Ceremonies has been at work. Christ, who said to the disciples "Ye have not chosen me, but I have chosen you," can truly say to every group of Christian friends "You have not chosen one another but I have chosen you for one another." The Friendship is not a reward for our discrimination and good taste in finding one another out. It is the instrument by which God reveals to each the beauties of all the others. They are no greater than the beauties of a thousand other men; by Friendship God opens our eyes to them. They are, like all beauties, derived from Him, and then, in a good Friendship, increased by Him through the Friendship itself, so that it is His instrument for creating as well as for revealing. At this feast it is He who has spread the board and it is He who has chosen the guests. It is He, we may dare to hope, who sometimes does, and always should, preside. Let us not reckon without our Host.

C.S. LEWIS, *THE FOUR LOVES*

> *I know not whether our names will be immortal; I am sure our friendship will.*
> WALTER SAVAGE LANDOR

Friends reveal God to each other because faith sharing is an important element of Christian friendship. Addressing His disciples in the context of the Last Supper, Jesus tells them, "I call you friends because I have made known to you everything I have learned from my father" (John 15:15). Here we see what constitutes a friendship is the intimacy of sharing that takes place in the relationship. As Jesus put it, "I shall not call you servants any more, because a servant does not know his master's business" (v. 15). Jesus honors his disciples as friends precisely by sharing the contents of His communication with God. Sharing one's religious experience and faith is central to Christian friendship.

WILKIE AU,
By Way of the Heart

Human love and the delights of friendship, out of which are built the memories that endure, are also to be treasured up as hints of what shall be hereafter.

BEDE JARRETT

A faithful friend can help us understand God's love. . .

Some friendships are based on having external things in common; when the circumstances in our lives change, the friendships start to fade. No longer nourished by common ground, they finally disappear.

But other friends hold on through all the changes. Like my friend Kathy.

I met her when we both taught at the same school years ago; to our surprise we discovered we were also neighbors. We both were married, but neither of us had children yet, and our lives ran parallel. For the next two years we shared laughter and sympathy as we carpooled to work every day.

Today, though, Kathy's still a teacher while I make my living tapping out words on the computer. She can never quite believe that I love what I do now far more

We need not set out in search for a friend. . . rather, we must simply set out to be the friend Christ modeled—anticipating the needs of others, wearing ourselves out at giving. Jesus died doing it.
JOY MACKENZIE

than I ever did teaching. We live on opposite sides of a small city these days, and our lives no longer run parallel. I wouldn't have been surprised if our friendship had faded away like so many others from my teaching days.

But Kathy's stubborn. She doesn't give up on me, even if our lives are different now. When I'm in trouble, she's always there to help, baby-sitting for my kids, bringing food and comfort, lending me her strength. When I need to hear the truth, she's not afraid to tell it to me; when I need someone to listen, she always cares. She loves my children, and helps me be a better mother. She loves my husband, and dares yell at him when he starts to take me for granted. We laugh with each other and hug each other, and we're always on each other's side.

Kathy's friendship is one of the reliable things in my life. When I think of her strong, beautiful face, I know I'm catching a glimpse of God.

Dear God, thank You for all my faithful friends. Their understanding, their forgiveness, their love all help me comprehend Your love a little more. Thank You for showing me Yourself through them. May they see You in me. Amen.

Holy Friendship that has medicine for all the wretchedness
is not to be despised. From God it truly is, that amid
the wretchedness of this exile, we be comforted
with the counsel of friends until we come to Him.

RICHARD ROLLE

*At that day
ye shall know
that I am in my Father,
and ye in me,
and I in you.*
JOHN 14:20 (KJV)

Our Heavenly Friend

I no longer call you servants. . . .
Instead, I have called you friends, for everything that I learned
from my Father I have made known to you.
JOHN 15:15 (NIV)

I'm not comfortable thinking of God as my buddy or pal, "The Big Guy Upstairs." After all, He's the Creator of the universe–and He is far beyond my ability to ever comprehend. And yet the Bible makes clear that God longs to have an intimate relationship with us. He doesn't want to be merely worshipped from afar; He wants to know and be known. The Bible uses metaphor after metaphor to show us the intimacy we can have with God: lover, shepherd, the vine, our father. . .our friend. My closest human relationship can only give me a glimpse of the union I have with Christ in my heart.

> *Love Him, and keep Him for thy Friend, who, when all go away, will not forsake thee, nor suffer thee to perish at the last.*
>
> THOMAS Á KEMPIS

Some days God's friendship seems more real to me than others. He never calls me on the phone or drops by for coffee or writes me a letter–and I'm so easily distracted from our friendship by my life's ordinary trivial concerns. But one day I will know Him even as I am known. . .and I will see clearly then what a good Friend He has been to me my whole life long.

For now we see through a glass, darkly;
but then face to face: now I know in part;
but then shall I know even as also I am known.

1 CORINTHIANS 13:12 (KJV)

*That I may know him, and the power of his resurrection,
and the fellowship of his sufferings. . . .*

PHILIPPIANS 3:10 (KJV)

God is the best friend because. . .

- He always understands.
- He's never too busy to listen.
- we can never be separated from His love.
- He knows us better than we know ourselves.
- He loves us more than anyone else ever could.

Have you ever had a friend whom you loved so much that you wanted to be with him all the time and get to know him better every day? . . . Jesus wants that kind of relationship with you.
FLORENCE LITTAUER,
PERSONALITY PLUS

Jesus had a remarkable way of being a friend to every person He met. We sense in Him the ability to welcome the stranger, to find the hidden gift in those others called sinners, to strengthen the ability of the loving to love more. He loved some by confronting them with the ways they were unloving and exploitive of others. He challenged the hypocritical. . . . He found important ways to invite all to discover and cherish the lovable in themselves. No one left Jesus less than they were when they came to Him. He spoke plainly and directly, but never destructively. Those who could hear Jesus' message left Him with a greater love for themselves, with a clearer sense of direction for their lives, and with a renewed awareness of God's unfailing love. Those who could not hear the message left Him angry and resentful yet confronted with the truth of their lives.

PAULA RIPPLE,
CALLED TO BE FRIENDS

The very possibility
of friendship
with God
transfigures life.
HENRY CHURCHILL KING

The purpose of prayer is to leave us alone with God.
LEO BAECK

With so good a Friend. . .ever present,
Himself the first to suffer, everything can be borne.
He helps, He strengthens, He never fails, He is the true Friend.
TERESA OF AVILA

I wouldn't expect my friendships with my earthly friends to last very long if I never communicated with them. For our friendships to grow, we need to talk, sharing our hearts, exchanging ideas; we need to spend time together. Sometimes I forget that the same applies to my relationship with God: If I never talk to Him, I can't expect my relationship with Him to grow.

I don't know how prayer works; I'm not sure of all the theological ramifications. But I do know that talking to God keeps me healthy—emotionally as well as spiritually (and some research even seems to indicate that prayer makes us physically healthier as well). We can try to analyze how prayer works, just as we might analyze why our bodies need to breathe—or we can forget about the whys and hows, and talk to God as simply and constantly as we breathe.

Our friendship with Him depends on it.

There is not in the world a kind of life more sweet and delightful than that of a continual conversation with God.

BROTHER LAWRENCE

Prayer should be more than a shopping list that we drop off with God. Real intimacy goes both ways.

What is the sign of a friend? . . .the last mark of intimacy is to confide secret joys. Have we ever let God tell us any of His joys, or are we telling God our secrets so continually that we leave no room for Him to talk to us? At the beginning of our Christian life we are full of requests to God, then we find that God wants to get us into a relationship with Himself, to get us in touch with His purposes. Are we so wedded to Jesus Christ's idea of prayer—"Thy will be done"—that we catch the secrets of God? The things that make God dear to us are not so much His great big blessings as the tiny things, because they show His amazing intimacy with us; He knows every detail of our individual lives.

OSWALD CHAMBERS

Prayer is God's own psychotherapy for His sinful children.
RAPHAEL SIMON

The secret friendship of the Lord
is with them that fear Him.
PSALM 25:14 (RV)

One way to easily keep your mind
focused during prayer,
and in greater peace, is to not let
it wander too far
[from God]
during the rest of the day.
BROTHER LAWRENCE

There is a friend that sticketh
closer than a brother.
PROVERBS 18:24 (KJV)

He doesn't ask much of us, just a thought of Him every now and then, a little adoration, sometimes a prayer for His grace, sometimes to offer Him your pain, at other times to thank Him for all that He has done for you in the past, and is still doing for you even now. . . and as often as you can com-

fort yourself with Him. Lift up your heart to Him, sometimes when you're eating or when people are around you; even the smallest thought will please Him. You don't need to cry very loudly; He is nearer to us than we think.

You don't need to be in church all the time to be with God. We can make a prayer chapel in our hearts where we can go from time to time to talk with Him, peacefully, humbly, lovingly. Everyone is capable to some degree of having this kind of familiar conversation with God. He knows what we are capable of. So let's get started.

BROTHER LAWRENCE,
THE PRACTICE OF THE PRESENCE OF GOD

1. TCHAIKOVSKY: Song Without Words (02:45) *Performed by Klaus Heidlemann and Vladamir Prevost*
2. HAYDN: Scherzo from Op. 33, No.4 in 'B' flat major (02:29) *Performed by the Bel Canto Quartet (Leader Antonio Vezey)*
3. HAYDN: Finale (Rondo) from Op. 33, No.3 in 'C' major (02:48) *Performed by the Bel Canto Quartet (Leader Antonio Vezey)*
4. FAURÉ: Berceuse (03:16) *Performed by Klaus Heidlemann and Vladamir Prevost*
5. HAYDN: Menuetto from Op. 77, No.2 in 'F' major (04:37) *Performed by the Bel Canto Quartet (Leader Antonio Vezey)*
6. VIVALDI: "Winter," Slow Movement (01:53) *Performed by the London Baroque Consort, conducted by André Pavanne*
7. CHOPIN: Waltz in 'A' flat (03:53) *Performed by Klaus Heidlemann and Sarah Heidlemann*
8. HAYDN: Andante from Op. 77, No.2 in 'F' major (06:57) *Performed by the Bel Canto Quartet (Leader Antonio Vezey)*
9. CHAUSSON: Le Colibri (03:05) *Performed by Klaus Heidlemann and Vladamir Prevost*
10. BIZET: Petit Mari, Petite Femme (02:07) *Performed by Klaus Heidlemann and Sarah Heidlemann*
11. MOZART: Menuetto from K387 in 'G' major (07:23) *Performed by the Bel Canto Quartet (Leader Antonio Vezey)*
12. GRIEG: Holberg Suite, "Gavotte" (03:52) *Performed by the London Baroque Consort, conducted by André Pavanne*
13. HAYDN: Menuetto from Op. 76, No.5 in 'D' major (02:56) *Performed by the Bel Canto Quartet (Leader Antonio Vezey)*
14. GRIEG: Holberg Suite, "Rigaudon" (05:03) *Performed by the London Baroque Consort, conducted by André Pavanne*

TOTAL RUNNING TIME: (53:08)

riends
friend
riends
frien